Written by

D1461772

£5.50
UK only

HELLO THERE!

Below: *Katy travelled to Cyprus to join the Red Arrows and took the hot seat in the Team Leader's jet as they practised their fabulous formation flying.*

Welcome to our twenty-eighth Blue Peter book. It's very important because it marks our ruby anniversary – that's an incredible forty years of Blue Peter!

Way back on 16 October 1958, when Blue Peter first went out, who'd have thought that there would be over 3000 programmes, twenty-five different presenters, thirty-seven Appeals, eighteen pets, more than 150,000 different items and nearly one million Blue Peter badge winners. Phew! We're exhausted just thinking about it. And if you haven't won a Blue Peter badge yet – check out page 61 to find out how you can.

Blue Peter is the longest continuous-running children's TV programme in the world! And because this book is a special edition, we also travel back in time and look at Blue Peter over the last four decades. See how many presenters and pets you and your family can recognise on pages 6–7 and 10–11.

It's impossible to squeeze all the best BP bits into one book but we do hope some of your favourites are included. Try your hand at a Blue Peter make, put on your apron and cook up a storm, and re-live some of our thrilling adventures on land, at sea and up in the air! All this and much, much more ...

Konnie Hq

This snow, which filled the Blue Peter garden, didn't fall from the sky. It was created by mixing air, water and a secret ingredient – liquid nitrogen. Fancy building snowmen all year round?

Stuart Miles

Richard met Oliver Hewitt and his classmates in North Wales. Oliver won our tennis shirt design competition and his fantastic prize was a tennis lesson from Britain's ace Tim Henman.

Richard Bacon

Katy and Richard earned their cup of tea when they joined tea pickers in Darjeeling during their trip to commemorate India's fiftieth anniversary of independence.

PAST & PRESENT

1958

⭐ Twenty-five-year-old Christopher Trace and twenty-one-year-old Leila Williams were the first Blue Peter presenters. Playing with train sets or dressing up dolls was about as exciting as it got during the fifteen-minute programme, transmitted once a week.

1967

⭐ Valerie Singleton replaced Leila in 1962 and John Noakes joined the programme in 1966, followed by Peter Purves in 1967. Val, John and Pete were a long-standing trio, as were their three four-legged friends.

1972

⭐ When Val left in 1972 to make her Blue Peter Special Assignment series, Lesley Judd, an ex-dancer with The Young Generation, joined the team and became Blue Peter's Action Girl.

1979

⭐ At the end of the 1970s, Simon Groom replaced Peter. A few months later Christopher Wenner joined, followed in 1979 by Tina Heath, making up the new trio pictured here. Tina left to have a baby in 1980, when Sarah Greene took over and Peter Duncan replaced Christopher.

⭐ Yet more changes in the Blue Peter team. By 1986, the trio still comprised Janet Ellis but she was now presenting the programmes with Mark Curry and Caron Keating.

1984

⭐ Janet Ellis became the sixth girl presenter when Sarah Greene left for Saturday Superstore. Soon after, Michael Sundin came to join Janet and Simon.

1986

⭐ At eighteen years old, Yvette Fielding was the youngest BP presenter when she arrived in 1987. She was joined by John Leslie in 1989 and Diane-Louise Jordan in 1990.

1990

⭐ No doubt the faces are now becoming familiar. Yes, they belong to Tim, Katy Hill, Stuart Miles and Romana D'Annunzio … and I think you know all about 1998!

1996

1993

⭐ Blue Peter revealed its latest trio of presenters. Anthea Turner replaced Yvette and Tim Vincent took over from John Leslie while Diane still remained on board.

Blue Peter in the

Blue Peter has always risen to a snowy sporting challenge. In years gone by, veteran John Noakes braved the two-man bobsleigh and got bruises to prove it. Years later, John Leslie pushed to even greater heights when ski jumping. Following in a long line of BP daredevils, Stuart Miles took on the ultimate test of human nerve – the Cresta Run.

Set in the Swiss Alps at the glamorous ski resort of St Moritz, the Cresta is a three-quarter-mile ice chute that twists and plunges down a mountain-side. The brave hurl themselves head first down the run on a toboggan at speeds of up to 80 m.p.h. The Cresta was first built in 1885 by a group of British thrillseekers who came each year to test their daring against local challengers. The British have remained to this day.

It was 7 o'clock in the morning, dark and freez-ing cold when Stuart arrived to take on the Cresta. "I've got butterflies in my stomach but there's no going back now," he called out as he went in to get kitted out with helmet, goggles and body protection. The safety briefing was a grisly list of

the injuries that have occurred on the Cresta and did nothing to steady nerves! After receiving instruction on how to lie, turn and – more to the point – brake, it was time to tackle the world-famous run.

snow

Finally, Stuart's name was called. He stepped carefully on to the ice and lay face down on the toboggan. The bell sounded and he edged forwards, slowly at first, then gathering speed fast – very fast. In moments the noise of blades on ice was deafening, as white walls flashed past in a blur. After negotiating the last turn he thundered on to the straight. Moments later he was at the bottom.

"Wow, that was amazing," he shouted breathlessly. "I've never experienced anything like that. After Shuttlecock corner I let it go – I couldn't begin to describe the sensation." He made a good time too – 69 seconds. Another BP victory!

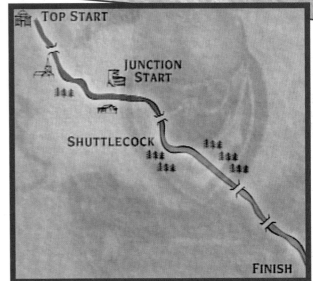

Top: *Stuart and Katy take to the slopes for a gentle ski the day before Stuart's big downhill toboggan challenge.*
Centre: *Beginners start the Cresta Run at "Junction" rather than "Top" – but that doesn't mean the experience is any less nerve-racking.*

Left: *Stuart receives last-minute tips from his Cresta tutor on how to negotiate the various twists and turns in the death-defying course for the first time.*
Above: *Stuart successfully takes on the notoriously dangerous Shuttlecock corner. From the moment the toboggan blades start moving on the ice, the sensation of speed is incredible.*

Blue Peter is a unique television programme in that it has four-legged members of the team.

The first Blue Peter pet joined way back in January 1963 – a black-and-brown mongrel puppy, whom viewers named Petra. She was to become a dog for everyone – those who just loved animals and those who couldn't have a dog of their own. She appeared on every programme and, when the presenters were filming, Petra went too. Petra was loved by millions of children and was part of Blue Peter until she was sadly put to sleep at the grand age of fourteen.

In 1965 Petra had eight puppies. One pup called Patch was kept and when John Noakes joined the following year, he became Patch's master. Tragedy struck in 1971 when, after a sudden illness, Patch died. He was replaced by a border collie called Shep. When John left the programme in 1978 it was only fair that Shep went with him.

Goldie, a beautiful seven-week-old golden retriever, was the next canine to join the team. Once again her name was chosen by the viewers and she lived with presenter Simon Groom. Goldie had two litters. All the first became guide dogs for the blind.

From the second litter, born 3 February 1986, Blue Peter kept Bonnie who was trained first by Janet Ellis then Yvette Fielding, but her best friend was Anthea Turner.

Mabel joined in 1996, completing our canine line-up of the past forty years of Blue Peter.

Now for the felines. In 1964 Jason, a seal point Siamese, became Blue Peter's first cat. He lived

Top: *Peter Purves, Valerie Singleton and John Noakes with dogs Petra and Patch, Jason the Siamese cat and Barney the parrot.*
Above: *Simon Groom and Goldie were inseparable during their ten years on the programme.*
Left: *Shep, another keen member of the BP team.*

Left: *Willow was on the programme for five years before she went to live in the country.* Above: *Kari and Oke are our current cats. Oke loves making friends and sitting on your lap. Kari, the female, prefers investigating the studio to sitting on her cushion.*

until January 1976 and was followed by twin silver tabbies named Jack and Jill. They became known as "disappearing cats" as they were always leaping out of presenters' arms and jumping off seats. Jill died in 1983 and Jack unexpectedly three years later.

In September 1986 Willow, a Balinese variant, was given to the programme. Willow wasn't so keen on coming to the studio so she retired to the country. She is still alive and well.

Our latest cats Kari and Oke were part of an abandoned litter cared for by the Wood Green Animal Shelter. In 1991 Blue Peter was glad to give them a caring home and cosy cushions in the studio. They are also different because they are not pedigree cats.

Tortoises are very much associated with Blue Peter, too. In 1963 our first tortoise, Fred, appeared. He was later renamed Freda when it was pointed out that "he" was in fact a "she". In spring 1979 we discovered she had not survived in hibernation, so Maggie and Jim – hatched from their eggs in Leicester – were given to the programme. They survived until the abnormally cold January of 1982. New government regulations banning the mass importation of tortoises to Britain meant that it was difficult to replace Maggie and Jim. Blue Peter wanted to continue to show how tortoises should be properly cared for and were

delighted when George was offered. When not hibernating, George is full of life and enjoys nothing more than a good scramble around the Blue Peter garden.

That almost brings the Blue Peter pets up to date – unless you know someone with a very long memory. Yes, the programme even had parrots as pets. Joey, the first parrot, was followed by Barney but sadly neither bird lived long and since then parrots haven't appeared as Blue Peter pets.

Below: *George is the liveliest tortoise we know. He races around the Blue Peter garden and particularly enjoys eating fresh lettuce, which Clare the gardener always grows for him.*

Marvellous Mabel!

In January 1996 the Royal Society for the Prevention of Cruelty to Animals phoned to tell us that since Christmas many more abandoned and ill-treated animals had been taken into care. The RSPCA wanted us to remind viewers that a pet is not just for Christmas but also for life ...

F our sorry specimens were brought into the Blue Peter studio and we could hardly believe their sad stories. Two black ducks had been found horribly chained and left in a yard – all they needed was a pond to make them happy and several people in our office thought they knew a suitable one. A cute kitten had been abandoned in a carrier bag – our camera supervisor was desperate to give him a new home. And as for the perky, little,

six-month-old, black-and-white pup – well, we all had our eye on her!

She'd been found starving and very close to death before RSPCA Inspector Mark Buggy rescued her. She was christened Mabel because Mark had chalked his initials MAB on kennel number one. It was later misread as Mabel. The name stuck and is now known to millions of Blue Peter viewers.

Mabel is a border collie cross with one blue eye and one brown. If she had a passport, another identifying feature would be her famous floppy ear. She officially joined the programme on 19 February 1996 and fortunately Bonnie didn't mind sharing the limelight with another four-legged female.

Mabel loves Bonnie and enjoys coming with her to Television Centre every Monday, Wednesday and Friday afternoon. She immediately got a reputation as a tearaway and she runs rings around the camera crew – to say nothing of the rest of us! Mabel enjoys meeting all our guests, although we've discovered she doesn't like clowns

Left: Celebrity guest Rolf Harris with Mabel – they took an instant shine to each other!

with big feet, or very loud noises. Another thing she doesn't like is sharing the studio with strange dogs – particularly other females. She's very territorial and protective – probably her sheepdog instincts coming out.

The highlight of Mabel's day is a really good romp with her ball in the park. She has lots of furry friends that she regularly plays with: Flora, Lillemann, Barney, Oscar, Max and Percy – the only dog who runs faster than Mabel! In the summer,

though, she loves to swim and is reluctant to come out of the water until she's absolutely exhausted.

We don't know exactly how old Mabel is so she has an "official" birthday (just like Her Majesty the Queen) on the same day as Bonnie – that is, on 3 February. Our lucky birthday girls receive loads of lovely home-made cards, which we display in the studio, and then they wolf down the ultimate treat – a slice of delicious doggie cake! Many happy returns Mabel (and Bonnie, of course).

Mabel
by
John Hegley
(Poet/Comedian)

What kind of dog is Mabel?
She's a dog that has some fur.
What kind of dog's a table?
Very different from her.
It cannot sniff, its legs are stiff,
It can't run round the park,
It has no food, it's made of wood
but hasn't got a bark.
The table unlike Mabel is unable
to do a lot.
Is it an endangered species?
No, it's not.

Left: Katy with Bonnie, who becomes a teenager on her next birthday.

Top: Konnie making friends with Mabel on her first day as a Blue Peter presenter.
Above: Mabel enjoys a daily swim in Richmond Park when it is warm in summer.
Left: It's not often you find Mabel resting.

Born 20 February 1969

Height 1.8m

Home town Maidstone, Kent

Star sign Pisces

Sister Allison (16 months younger)

THE EARLY YEARS

School	Maidstone Grammar School
Best subjects	Music, drama, chemistry, art
Worst subject	Maths
Qualifications	9 O Levels, 3 A Levels, BA (Hons) in Media Production
Earliest ambition	To be a vet
First acting experience	Playing Joseph in a nativity play
Hobbies when younger	Duke of Edinburgh award scheme, kept stick insects and creepy-crawlies, magic, guitar, singing, Cadet force
Pets when younger	Dusty, a dog; stick insects, spiders etc
First job	On a farm – bean grading

STUART MILES

"I've had so many adventures since joining Blue Peter in June 1994," says Stuart, "that it wasn't easy to pick out just a couple of my favourite highlights. Our 1997 Summer Expedition to Canada is definitely on the list. In this very enjoyable trip to a country full of contrasts we visited exciting cities like Toronto as well as the magnificent Rocky Mountains. Spotting and tracking a mother bear with her cubs from a helicopter was fantastic."

There's no doubt about what Stuart sees as his greatest achievement on the programme. "Being the first civilian to take part in a free-fall display at the Biggin Hill Air Show in 1997 makes me very proud. I can still remember how I felt, having just landed, taking my parachute off in a hurry, ready to stand in line as an RAF Hercules flew past in salute over our heads. It still makes my spine tingle!"

Stuart's other great memory was when he was charged by an elephant. "The moment when I thought my career and everything was over was in Kenya with the Born Free Foundation helping to relocate an elephant called Tembo. Having been transported in a box for twenty-four hours, Tembo was angry when he came out and so charged our landrover. Fortunately the five ton elephant moved off into the bush when our driver turned on the car engine."

And which Blue Peter team does Stuart remember watching the most? "Like many people, it was Val, John and Pete. They also had trouble with an elephant once – it must be something about being a Blue Peter presenter."

FAVOURITE THINGS

Colour	Blue
Best food	Ice-cream (preferably chocolate)
Worst food	Brussels sprouts
Sports	Tennis, swimming, parachuting
Band	Manic Street Preachers
Album	"Everything Changes" by Manic Street Preachers
TV shows	EastEnders, This Life, The X-Files
Star	Zoë Ball
Best film	Romeo and Juliet
Clothes	Combat trousers
Best ways to spend Saturdays	Cinema, gym, watch some football on TV, spend as much money as possible!

MORE FACTS

Car	Alfa Romeo Spider
Most wants to do on BP	Parachute over the North Pole, swim with dolphins
Bad habit	Used to bite my nails
Country most wants to visit	Australia
People most respect	People who follow their dreams
Ambition	To follow my own dreams

In 1996 the Blue Peter Great Bring and Buy Sale was to raise money for people suffering from "the world's oldest disease", leprosy – or Hansen's disease as it is properly known. Although it does not normally occur in Britain, many people have heard of leprosy and are shocked to think that millions of people around the world have this terrible disease. It particularly effects people in countries around the Equator including Brazil and India.

Stuart travelled to Brazil to meet some of the people – both young and old – who have leprosy and suffer physically and emotionally as they will often be rejected by friends and family. He met fourteen-year-old Adriana, who told him, "My friends treat me badly, they say awful things to me. They make me feel like an outcast."

Fortunately leprosy can be cured with drugs and, if diagnosed early enough, there will be no lasting physical effects at all. That message was well and truly received by Blue Peter viewers, who held Bring and Buy sales in their thousands. Having broken through the first target of £500,000 and a second target of £1,500,000 by June 1996, the final total was £2,800,000 – a truly amazing result.

Working with the charity Lepra, we now had enough money to provide mobile treatment units with twenty-eight jeeps, thirty-two motorbikes and 118 bicycles as well as a new leprosy clinic in Ceara, Brazil and a new laboratory and operating treatment unit in Hyderabad, India. These projects would be funded over five years, making it possible to cure around 80,000 people of leprosy – all thanks to Blue Peter viewers.

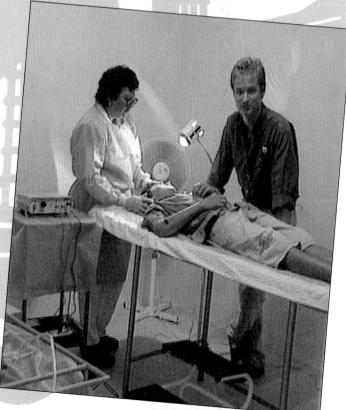

out all over Britain

In October 1997 Stuart went back to Brazil for the official opening ceremony of the Blue Peter leprosy clinic at Ceara. Among all the happy faces on that day, said Stuart, one smile shone out above all others. In less than a year Adriana's life had completely changed for the better now that the clinic was treating her.

The subject of our 1997 Appeal, which was for people in Britain, was introduced to us in a film by thirteen-year-old Kelly, who lives in Cambridge. Like some 7000 other people in this country, Kelly has cystic fibrosis – a disease you can't catch, you are born with it. Cystic fibrosis affects the lungs, creating a sticky mucus that makes it difficult to breathe.

Kelly told us what she has to do every single day to keep herself well. She starts early, at 6.40 a.m., with her mum helping her with physiotherapy to loosen her lungs. Then it's fifteen minutes on a nebuliser – a machine that vaporises the liquid in her lungs. With every meal there is a cocktail of antibiotics and medicines to prevent infection and aid digestion. There's more physio and nebulising in the evening after school but no complaints from Kelly. At her school she enjoys activities such as swimming and gym – they just take a bit more effort than for other people.

Working with the Cystic Fibrosis Trust, the 1997 Blue Peter Appeal aimed to provide portable equipment: nebulisers, oxygen kits and trampolines, several special mobile cystic fibrosis nurses and new cystic fibrosis day-care centres.

Bring and Buy sales had proved so popular the year before that we thought we'd try them again – and we weren't disappointed. Once again an initial target of £500,000 was achieved in early January 1998 and by June had reached £2,048,000 as Blue Peter viewers put on Bring and Buy sales in their thousands.

Opposite top: *Katy with our genie Totaliser showing £1,000,000 raised by 30 January 1998 for the Blue Peter Appeal for Cystic Fibrosis.*
Opposite centre: *The first Blue Peter four-wheel-drive vehicle being delivered to a Leprosy Control Programme in Orissa, India.*
Opposite far left: *Stuart meets children in Juazeiro Do Norte, Brazil.*
Opposite left: *Stuart with the first patient to receive treatment in the newly refurbished Dona Libania Clinic in Fortaleza, Brazil.*

Many thanks to everyone who's held a Blue Peter Bring and Buy sale. They really have made a great difference to thousands of people's lives, and work carried out by the charities concerned will continue for several years.

Top: *Having your face painted with a Blue Peter ship was popular at some Bring and Buy sales.*
Below: *Richard with pupils at his old primary school in Mansfield, which supported the Appeal.*
Bottom: *A letter and photo of their Bring and Buy sale sent by Blue Peter viewers Joshua and Emily.*

Skydiving with the Falcons, underwater escape training strapped into a submerged aircraft or pulling 4g while testing out the latest hair-raising theme-park attraction are all in a day's work as a Blue Peter presenter. However just occasionally a challenge comes along that is both exciting and enjoyable. Travelling to Château d'Oex in Switzerland to take part in the prestigious David Niven Cup balloon race was one of those occasions, and Katy was the lucky passenger.

The race is named after the famous actor David Niven, who was a big ballooning fan, and is the "Grand Prix" of the ballooning world, in which the crème de la crème test their endurance and prove their navigating skills. The race rules allow each team the same quantity of fuel and the winner is the balloon that travels the farthest.

Flying a balloon is tricky at the best of times but add to that navigating between the highest mountains in Europe as well as unpredictable weather and you've got an even hairier challenge. Katy's adventure began the day before the race at the safety briefing where she met her pilot Robin Batchelor.

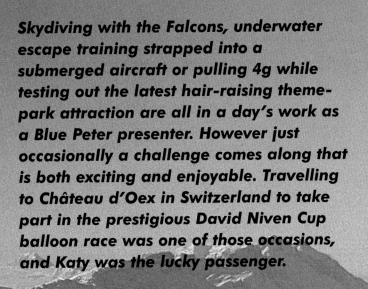

THE SKY'S THE LIMIT!

Above: A chair balloon – great for taking in mountain views.
Left: The triumphant team pose for photos after their safe landing in a farmer's field.

Above: *Katy and pilot Robin Batchelor admire the view.*
Left: *Minus 10°C outside, but Katy's keeping warm while taking charge of the brazier.*

Bright and early the next morning the contestants were busy preparing for the race. Everywhere people were unrolling and inflating the thirty balloons in the competition – the brilliant orange flames from the heaters took the chill off the morning air.

Very soon it was time for the start, which was signalled by a gun shot. The sight of so many balloons taking off together in the early morning light was breathtaking. "Coming through the clouds into brilliant blue sky was totally awesome," says Katy, who clearly relished the experience. "All you can see for miles is an ocean of cloud with the odd mountain peak poking through. It's so peaceful."

When flying at altitudes of around 5000 metres, the air gets pretty thin and that can have a strange effect on your head so the crew tested each other's concentration every few minutes with simple times-table questions. It's not a good idea to lose your marbles while in control of an aircraft three miles up in the sky …

Katy's balloon drifted over the border into France. All too soon it began to lose altitude and three hours after the start of the race it touched down in a field in the French countryside. Well, they may not have come first – or second or third for that matter – but, as they sat down to the lunch prepared by the farmer whose field they'd landed in, that didn't seem to matter!

Born	15 April 1971
Height	1.7m
Home town	Brentwood, Essex
Star sign	Aries
Brother/Sister	Simon (aged 28), Naomi (aged 19)

THE EARLY YEARS

School	St Edward's Comp., Chadwell Heath
Best subjects	English, biology, German, CDT (Craft, Design & Technology)
Worst subjects	Maths (especially algebra), physics
Qualifications	9 0 Levels, 4 A Levels
Earliest ambition	To present Blue Peter!
First acting experience	Played Mary in primary school nativity play
Hobbies when younger	Riding, swimming, making perfume from rose petals
Pets when younger	Hammy, a hamster; Fluff, a rabbit; Flair and Cilla, horses; Blackie, Mowgli and Tigger, cats
First job	In a record shop

Presenting KATY HILL

"I've known what I wanted to do since I was five," says Katy. "Most people thought I was mad and believed it was a hopeless dream, although my parents were very supportive. The careers officer at school wanted me to be an optician." Luckily for us, Katy realised her childhood ambition in June 1995.

My most extraordinary adventure on Blue Peter so far was spending five days in Mongolia. I lived with a family in a yurt, sleeping, cooking and eating as they do on the Mongolian plains. When it came to saying goodbye it was very difficult because I had become close to the family even though I couldn't speak a word of Mongolian. I was given a ring by the grandmother of the family, which I still have. It was a very special moment."

Katy doesn't hesitate when it comes to her most nerve-racking assignment. "Without question it was underwater survival training with the Royal Navy Air Arm at Yeovilton in Somerset. Being strapped upside down in your seat in a helicopter simulator filled with water is no joke. It's so disorientating – even when you finally manage to release your harness you're not entirely sure which way is up, and the swim to the surface feels like it's never going to end! Then, when you think the nightmare is over, you have to do it again!"

A week on Blue Peter is always packed with lots of variety. "One week I was in the studio on Monday, when the programme included a film of me training with top rally car driver Juha Kankkunen, and in the next programme I chatted to Nick Park OBE, creator of Wallis and Grommit. That evening I flew off to Dusseldorf to film with Cirque du Soleil. I arrived back at 8 a.m. in time to rehearse Friday's live programme, including playing cricket with the England women's team."

FAVOURITE THINGS

Colour	Red
Best foods	Italian, I love it!
	I also *love* broad beans
Worst food	Liver and kidney
Sports	Riding, tennis, diving, driving
Bands	Garbage, Alisha's Attic, Alanis Morisette
Album	"Jagged Little Pill" by Alanis Morisette
TV shows	Friends, They Think It's All Over
Stars	Brad Pitt, Leonardo Di Caprio
Best films	Pretty Woman, National Velvet, Roman Holiday
Clothes	Silver sundress (because I wear it when the weather's nice and summer is here)
Best ways to spend Saturdays	Sitting outside a street café watching the world go by, having a dinner party with my friends

MORE FACTS

Car	Porsche Boxter
Most wants to do on BP	Drive a Formula 1 car, get my pilot's licence
Bad habits	Spending too much time on the phone, reading newspapers over people's shoulders
Country most wants to visit	Morocco
People most respect	Anne Frank, my family
Ambitions	To visit every country in the world, to seize the moment and live life to the full so that I never have any regrets

animal hospital

Make your

YOU WILL NEED

Large, strong cardboard box
White card, paper or paint
Grey emulsion paint
Sticky-backed plastic (optional)
Stick-type glue • 2 Large beads
Brass paper fasteners • 2 Tissue boxes
Small yoghurt or fromage-frais tub for sink
Silver model paint
2 Cable clips • Cork
Pieces of thin card for doors etc
2 Washing-up liquid bottles
Cardboard tube, 12cm long
Small amounts of felt or other material for cushions and pet blankets
Small boxes for animal cages and carrying-box (a light bulb box makes a good medium-sized cage)
Net mesh from fruit or nut bag
3 Small matchboxes
Various container and bottle tops for feeding bowls, dryers etc

The actual room

1 Cut away one side of the large cardboard box so that you are left with three "walls".

2 Cut off the top flaps from the box and fill in any large spaces on the "floor" to make it level.

3 Cover the walls with thin white card or paper, or paint them if you

prefer. Cover the floor with grey emulsion paint or sticky-backed plastic.

4 For the tiling, draw lines with a pencil and ruler on small sheets of white card. You can use the width of your ruler as a guide for the gaps between the lines to save time measuring out each space.

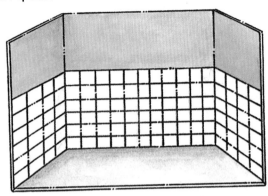

5 Glue the sheets of tiling around the walls.

6 For the door into the room, cut an oblong piece of card. Either cover it or paint it. Push a brass paper fastener through a bead for the door knob. Fix the knob through the door and spread out the pointed ends on the back.

7 Glue the door on to a slightly larger piece of card, which will show like a frame round the sides and top. Then fix the door and frame in place.

The base units

1 Cover the top, sides and front of one tissue box with card or white paint. (The open part of the box should be at the back of the unit where it won't show.)

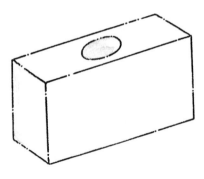

2 For the sink, wash out the yoghurt or fromage-frais tub well, then dry it.

3 Paint it silver or, if you prefer, leave it white.

4 Trim off the top edge of the tub to leave a small rim all round.

5 Place the tub rim upside down on top of one of the units and draw round it.

6 Cut away the cardboard a little way inside the

drawn line. Then gently insert the tub into the hole.

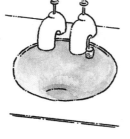

7 For the taps, push the nail end of each cable clip through the unit behind the sink opening. You can fit small pieces of cork over the nail ends to hold them in position.

8 For the doors, paint thin card or cover it with sticky-backed plastic. Push brass paper fasteners through the front of each door, and spread out the pointed ends on the back. Then glue the doors in place.

9 Make the second base unit in the same way but without the sink. One of the doors isn't needed either, since it is hidden in the corner by the first base unit.

The examination table and chair

1 For the table base, cut off the sloping top from one washing-up liquid bottle, making sure the cut is made evenly down the side.

2 For the table leg, push the cardboard tube over the table base, where the cap has fitted. Cut slits at intervals into the other end of the tube.

3 For the table top, paint an oblong piece of strong cardboard or cover it with sticky-backed plastic. Spread out the cut ends of the tube and glue them in the middle of the underside of the table top.

4 Make the chair base and leg in the same way as the table's.

5 Cut a washing-up liquid bottle down to the

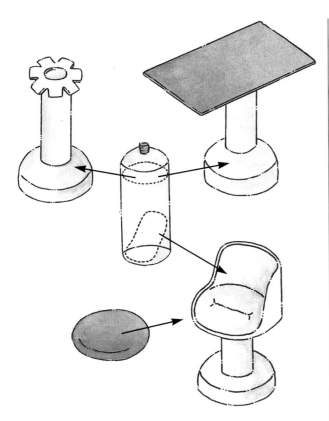

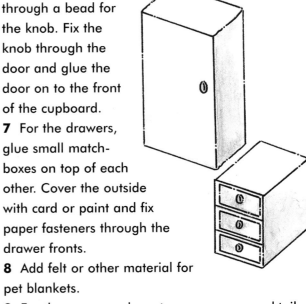

height you want your chair to be, then make the seat by cutting away at the front leaving the very bottom of the bottle as the seat.

6 Make a small cushion for the seat if you want.

The animal cages

1 Paint each box all over and seal up one end, leaving the other end open so that you can put an animal in.

2 For the front of the cage, cut away the main part of one side, leaving a small edge all round.

3 Draw and cut out a cardboard frame to fit over the cut edge.

4 For the wire mesh, cut out a piece of mesh slightly bigger than the frame. Spread glue on the inside of the frame and then press the edges of the mesh into the glue. You can pull the mesh edges either way if necessary to make the holes an even size.

5 Once the glue has dried, trim off the spare mesh around the edges. Paint the frame and glue it to the front of the box.

6 For the wall cupboard, cover a sardine tin packet with white card. Cover a separate piece of card for the door and push a brass paper fastener

through a bead for the knob. Fix the knob through the door and glue the door on to the front of the cupboard.

7 For the drawers, glue small match-boxes on top of each other. Cover the outside with card or paint and fix paper fasteners through the drawer fronts.

8 Add felt or other material for pet blankets.

9 For the mouse or hamster cage, use a cocktail-stick box. Cut up tissue paper for bedding.

The animal carrying-box

1 Reseal the end of a gravy cube box and then cut through the middle of one side. Cover with brown paper. Cut a slit in each end flap.

2 Cut out and cover small pieces of card with handles cut in them. Glue them to the box. Make tiny air holes in the box with a pencil point.

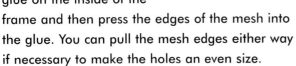

Other hospital accessories
- The frog or fish bowl is a clear top from a hairspray.
- The feeding bowl is a small jam container with the edge trimmed and painted.
- The brush is a toothbrush with the handle cut off.
- The stainless-steel bowl is the lower part of a two-sectioned yoghurt pot painted silver.
- The dryer is the nozzle from a hand-cream bottle, with thin elastic for a cord and the cap from a washing-up bottle for a plug. You can fix the "plug" to a square of card for an electric power point.
- The noticeboard is an oblong of white card or paper glued on top of a slightly larger black one. To make the scene even more lifelike, you can write notices or draw graphs to pin to the board.

Full steam ahead!

Our programme isn't the only Blue Peter institution celebrating in 1998. The 60532 Blue Peter is fifty years old. This Class A-2 Pacific Locomotive first went into service on 25 March 1948. She was withdrawn in 1966 but thanks to two railway enthusiasts, Geoff Drury and Brian Hollingsworth, she was saved from the scrap heap. In 1970, after being restored, the Blue Peter presenters of the day (Val, John and Pete) were proud to perform her naming ceremony, which was held in Doncaster where the loco was built. Sixty thousand people turned up to witness this momentous event.

To mark her fiftieth anniversary, the 532 Blue Peter undertook a unique journey, which was specially filmed. Carrying the programme's fortieth anniversary logo, the 532 travelled from Edinburgh's Waverley Station to London's King's Cross – the first time a steam locomotive has undertaken this 392-mile journey for thirty years. The epic trip took some fourteen hours. The loco's arrival at King's Cross was welcomed not only by a steel band but also by two former BP presenters, Valerie Singleton and John Noakes. Long may she steam on!

RICHARD BACON

Richard fulfilled his childhood ambition when he joined Blue Peter in February 1997. "I remember seeing Caron Keating filming with Blue Peter when I was on holiday with my family. I was about ten years old but I had dreams that it would be me one day. I couldn't believe it when I heard I'd got the job and I had to keep it secret for over a week. When I rang my mum she jumped up and down screaming with excitement."

Blue Peter was a big change from Richard's previous job with cable channel LiveTV. "On Blue Peter I've picked tea on a plantation in India, fished with some Inuits in northern Canada, had a lesson on being a clown with Cirque du Soleil in Germany, filmed at the Johnson Space Centre in Houston, Texas, and in Britain I've been dragon-boat racing, llama trekking, and trained with the English cricket team at Edgbaston. So all in all I'm having a ball."

THE EARLY YEARS

School	Worksop College
Best subjects	Physics, politics
Worst subject	RE
Qualifications	8 O Levels, 3 A Levels
Earliest ambition	To be an MP – but that was a long time ago
First acting experience	Convincing my Headmaster it wasn't me who set the fire alarm off
Hobbies when younger	Drums, piano, saxophone (rubbish at all of them!)
Pet when younger	Scamper, a Yorkshire Terrier
First job	McDonald's

FAVOURITE THINGS

Colour	Electric blue
Best food	Bread
Worst food	Sushi
Sports	Snooker, football
Bands	The Jam, Oasis, Ocean Colour Scene
Album	"Revolver" by The Beatles
TV shows	Anything with Steve Coogan in it
Star	Steve Coogan (man behind Alan Partridge)
Best films	Shawshank Redemption; *also like* Orson Wells films (Citizen Kane), Stars Wars
Clothes	Bright cheap shirts that *look* expensive
Best way to spend Saturdays	In bed

Born   30 November 1975
Height   1.85m
Home town   Mansfield, Nottinghamshire
Star sign   Sagittarius
Sisters   Juliet, Helena

MORE FACTS

Car	Honda CRX
Most wants to do on BP	Hang-gliding
Bad habits	Never ever tidy up, always late!
Country most wants to visit	China
People most respect	Good comedians e.g. Steve Coogan
Ambitions	To learn to cook, start to tidy up, be on time

RACING THE DRAGON

Richard was put through his paces when he went dragon-boat racing with the Royal Marines. First he had to train with them in Exeter, in Devon, to see if he was sufficiently fit and fast enough to join one of their official races. It certainly wasn't easy but Richard was determined to be part of the team.

The ancient art of dragon-boat racing dates back to the fourth century BC, when Quo Yuan, the minister of a much-loved Chinese emperor, drowned himself in the Mi Lo River in the Chinese kingdom of Chu. Legend has it that local

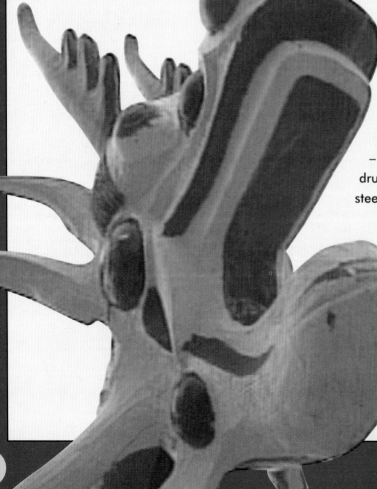

fishermen then raced out with their boats in an attempt to save him but failed. Then, to prevent his body being eaten by fish, they beat the water furiously with their paddles.

Dragon-boat races are a re-enactment of those fishermen's efforts and an annual festival in Hong Kong commemorates Quo Yuan's death. Fierce-looking dragon heads at the front of the long boats were added to ward off evil water spirits.

Dragon-boat racing is all about team work – there are eighteen or twenty paddlers and a drummer to keep everyone together, plus a steersman. The Royal Marines has one of the best dragon-boat teams in the UK, achieving over eighty-five strokes a minute to power the boat.

Fortunately for Richard, in training they start at a slow pace.

The dragon-boat racing season runs throughout the summer and the Marines' first official race meeting was at Salford Quays. Richard went along, hoping to take part in a race. The team successfully got through all the heats without Richard and reached the semi-finals – so would Richard be selected for this important race? "It was a tough decision but we know you've worked hard so we're going to put you in," said team manager Jed Stone.

"Great news – I won't let you down," replied Richard.

After some warming-up and stretching exercises it was time for a race briefing, where the stern advice from the team coach was, "what we want is lots of concentration, long hard stokes and keep in time with the paddle."

"I'm in trouble if I don't pull my weight," remarked Richard.

The race lasted just two minutes, the longest two minutes of Richard's life. The Royal Marine Dragon Slayers won the semi convincingly enough but outside their usual time. So would Richard make the final?

For the final Jed chose his A team of men, which didn't include Richard. His job would be cheering from the bank. Competing against three other teams in the final, the Royal Marines led

for most of the race but were just pipped at the post by the Hartlepool Powermen – there was only half a second between them. Perhaps if Richard had been in the Marines' team they would have won!

Above: *Richard and the crew do early morning training on the River Exe.*
Opposite: *Richard contemplates the challenge.*
Below: *Amid a great deal of sweat and competing dragon heads, three boats vie for victory at Salford Quays.*

Fridays – behind the scenes
CLEOPATRA

1.30 p.m. The girls arrive at BBC Television Centre in a minibus specially tailored to their many different needs.

1.50 p.m. Katy and Romana say "Hi" to the girls before they are whisked into the Blue Peter studio.

If it's Friday, there's probably pop on BP. But unlike a lot of other shows, we only have LIVE pop. The youngest and most impressive band to visit our studio in 1998 was Cleopatra. Lead vocals came from sixteen-year-old Cleopatra and backing vocals (BVs as they're called in the business) were provided by her two sisters Zainam and Yonah.

When we invited the talented trio from Manchester to perform their debut single "Cleopatra's Theme", they hadn't sung on any other TV programme.

While travelling between venues, the girls use their own minibus. You'd be amazed what it contains – classroom, canteen, computer games arcade, music studio and wardrobe – as well as providing room for their mum, manager, minder, tutor, to say nothing of their fab driver Gilbert.

It's a good job everyone gets on so well because the girls' day had started at a gruesome 3.30 a.m. – they'd been interviewed on a live breakfast show. An unexpected request from a news programme meant Cleopatra

didn't have time for lunch before they arrived in our studio 8 for a sound check and camera rehearsal.

During rehearsals, we were knocked out by the talented band but their manager, Tony Lovell, didn't smile until he was happy with the sound mix. Sandwiches and herbal teas were speedily

2.15 p.m. Floor manager, Simone, passes on messages to Cleopatra from the director. "Save the best performance for transmission."

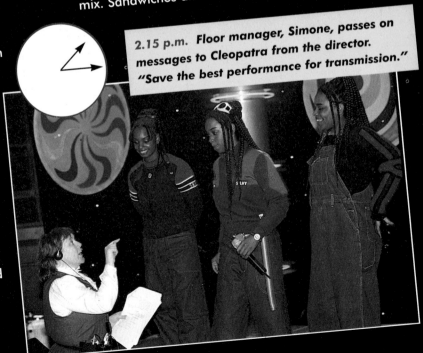

5.10 p.m. *Live on air – Cleopatra's music fills the studio and everyone knows they're witnessing a real star performance.*

grabbed from the tea bar (the girls like to eat as heathily as possible) and then it was a rush to make-up and wardrobe.

After it was all over, if you think the girls left our studio bound for a showbiz party, you'd be wrong. They might have had the invitation but when their mum said "early night" no one had the energy to complain.

4.35 p.m. *With a little help from Cleopatra's mum and Karen, the BP make-up designer, hair and make-up are given the full treatment.*

FACTFILE

Ages	Zainam 17, Cleopatra 16, Yonah 14
Home town	Moss Side in Manchester
Family	Terry, their ten-year-old sister. There'll be space for her if she wants to join the group when she's older
Musical heroes	Michael Jackson, Madonna, Spice Girls, Another Level, Gary Barlow
Ambitions	To fill Wembley Stadium, to conquer America
Clothes	Zainam spends most of her money on clothes and has a big influence on the group's image
Catch phrase	"Comin' Atcha" (Cleopatra)

The Blue Peter

1 The Blue Peter Summer Expedition of 1997 was to the second largest country in the world, what is its name?

2 Peter Duncan, John Leslie and Tim Vincent on different occasions all completed which running distance?

3 The Blue Peter theme tune has the same name as the first rock named by NASA scientists on the planet Mars, what is it?

4 There have been two Scottish presenters on Blue Peter, who were they?

5 What was the name of Bonnie's mother?

10 What kind of creature were Blue Peter pets Freda/Fred and George?

11 The first Blue Peter cat had the same name as a character in Greek mythology who was sent to collect the Golden Fleece. What was it?

12 Which former BP presenter regularly presents Crufts Dog Show?

6 Who was the Editor of Blue Peter for twenty-seven years from 1962 to 1988?

7 "Get down Shep" is a catch phrase associated with which presenter?

8 What kind of tree in the BP garden is the tree for the year 2000?

9 Who has been the longest-serving Blue Peter presenter to date?

13 The **famous elephant** that disgraced itself in front of Val, John and Pete had the same name as a well-known British singer, what was it?

14 **Blue Peter** is named after what?

15 In 1976 **Lesley Judd** was a passenger on the inaugural flight from London to Washington on which plane?

16 Which current presenter interviewed **Neil Kinnock** for Newsround prior to the 1992 General Election?

17 Stuart and Katy made a successful simultaneous **tandem parachute jump** to celebrate which Blue Peter milestone?

18 During the **Blue Peter Summer Expedition of 1993** Diane and Anthea visited the spectacular Iguazu Falls in which country?

19 Which ex-Blue Peter presenter went on to present **Saturday Superstore** and **Going Live?**

20 **Mansfield** is the family home of which current Blue Peter presenter?

Answers on page 62

Old houses are often full of strange stories about the people who used to live in them, as Konnie discovered when she went to Woburn Abbey in Bedfordshire on the trail of a remarkable woman called Mary du Caurroy Tribe.

Having married Herbrand Russell, younger son of the Duke of Bedford, Mary never expected to become a Duchess but her life changed for ever when her husband's older brother died. Mary and Herbrand left the remote and wild part of Scotland where they were living to take up residence at Woburn Abbey as the Duke and Duchess of Bedford.

The Duchess was a very active person who was unimpressed by wealth, grandeur and a life of leisure. She preferred outdoor activities, the countryside, animals and sport including mountaineering, ice skating and driving her own Rolls-Royce.

When Konnie visited Woburn she also went to the hospital that the Duchess opened there in order to do something useful with her life. The Duchess helped in many operations and became a skilled radiologist, conducting X-ray examinations at a time when this technique was still relatively new.

The Duchess however had health problems of her own and was slowly going deaf. Her ears were constantly filled with a noise she described as being like "railway trains rushing through stations". Her medical condition was probably what we now call "tinnitus". A

friend suggested that flying might help these "noises in the head", as Mary called them.

One afternoon in 1926, the sixty-one-year-old Duchess took to the air as a passenger in a tiny plane and circled over Woburn Abbey. Hearing a droning sound above them the staff rushed to the windows to see what it was. The plane circled several times because the Duchess would not let the pilot land until the last possible moment.

Mary was delighted to discover that the experiment had worked and that the change in air pressure relieved the terrible buzzing in her ears. She could also hear better against a background of noise. The Duchess soon became famous for her flying adventures and the press

Flying Duchess

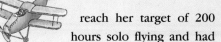

nicknamed her the Flying Duchess. She was even invited to talk about her new interest on the BBC radio service. It seemed that only the Duke disapproved of his wife's hobby.

Undeterred and not satisfied with being just a passenger, Mary learned to fly herself. She went on many pioneering trips including a record-breaking, eight-day flight to India, a seventeen-day round trip to South Africa and a dangerous trek across the Sahara desert. Her flights were not all without mishap. Once she narrowly escaped death when her plane was shot at by desert tribesmen, and on another occasion she was forced to crash land and walk through the jungle to find shelter in a native's hut. Amazingly she celebrated her seventieth birthday with a half-hour flight.

Unfortunately the "noises" in Mary's ears were getting worse and then her eyesight started to fail too. She was growing weary and said, "I want a real rest and fresh air and the birds and loneliness."

On 22 March 1937, the Duchess took off in her de Havilland Gypsy plane from Woburn. She was aiming to reach her target of 200 hours solo flying and had just fifty-five minutes more to do. Although she had planned her route in good weather, Mary was never seen again. Eleven days later, a strut from her plane was washed up at Yarmouth but to this day nobody knows what actually happened.

At Woburn there is a special room devoted to her memory, which Konnie visited. Called the Flying Duchess Room, it's crammed with personal reminders of her unique and colourful life. After her death, Mary's husband the Duke said, "It's not easy to show where lay the magic charm of her personality. One thing is certain – she never wished to be put on a pedestal. Her sense of humour was too keen and for all her cleverness she was too unaffected for any pose."

Opposite top: *Konnie in aviation gear of the period.*
Opposite left: *The real Duchess in her younger days – quite the belle of the ball.*
Below: *The real Duchess of Bedford in her de Havilland Gypsy plane.*
Top right: *Konnie as the Duchess of Bedford about to go out in her Rolls-Royce.*
Bottom right: *The Duchess wasn't afraid to get her hands dirty if need be.*

Presenting ★ ★ ★ ★ ★
KONNIE HUQ

THE EARLY YEARS

School	Notting Hill & Ealing High School, London
Best subject	Art
Worst subject	RE
Qualifications	9 GCSEs, 3 A Levels, BA (Hons) in Economics
Earliest ambition	To climb the stairs
First acting experience	Acting up!
Hobbies when younger	Riding my bike, drawing
Pets when younger	Fish in garden pond (which were eaten by next door's cat)
First job	Scooping ice-cream in Ealing Broadway Centre

K onnie was no stranger to children's television when she joined Blue Peter in December 1997. "I started my presenting career at the age of seventeen while I was still at school," says Konnie. But before, aged fourteen, Konnie was once a guest on Blue Peter with the National Youth Music Theatre. "I sang a solo and met Caron Keating, Yvette Fielding and John Leslie, and I got a Blue Peter badge." She also appeared on Newsround when she interviewed Neil Kinnock the week before the 1992 General Election.

Konnie seems to have been a Blue Peter toddler. "I've got incredibly early memories of John Noakes and Shep, and I remember vividly when Bonnie was born and when Tina Heath had her baby."

She auditioned for Blue Peter while she was presenting Channel 5's Milkshake, so what's been her top adventure since then? "Going to Universal Studios in Florida was a real treat, especially testing out the new Twister ride. It was great fun but also makes you think how terrifying it would be if you were caught up in a real tornado."

And what does Konnie look forward to on Blue Peter? "There are lots of things, but I would like to visit Bangladesh again where my family originally comes from, to see what life is really like there." Keep watching to see if Konnie's wish comes true.

FAVOURITE THINGS

Colour	Green (today!)
Best foods	Pasta, pavlova, ice-cream – to name but a few!
Worst food	BBC canteen food
Sports	Depends on whether I'm watching or participating
Bands	Garbage, The Prodigy, The Fun Loving Criminals
Album	"Everything Must Go" by Manic Street Preachers (but only at the moment because I go through phases)
TV shows	Friends (1st series), This Life, The Simpsons, EastEnders
Star	The North Star!
Best films	Trading Places, When The Cat's Away
Clothes	My new army trousers
Best way to spend Saturdays	With my friends

Born	17 July 1975
Height	1.6m
Home town	Ealing, London
Star sign	Cancer
Sisters	Rupa, Nutun

MORE FACTS

Car	Don't have one yet
Most wants to do on BP	Fly a helicopter or a plane
Bad habit	I'm the world's most impatient person
Countries most wants to visit	East Asia, Africa
People most respect	Trevor McDonald
Ambition	To be happy always

Past Summer Expeditions

When Blue Peter is off the air during July and August the presenters go on a Summer Expedition to explore foreign countries and make films to show what life is like in different parts of the world. Apart from one year (1986) they have taken place every year since 1965. These are the places that have been visited.

Mexico 1970

1965 Norway
1966 Singapore and Borneo
1967 Jamaica and New York
1968 Morocco
1969 Ceylon
1970 Mexico
1971 Iceland, Norway and Denmark
1972 Fiji, Tonga and San Francisco
1973 The Ivory Coast
1974 Thailand
1975 Turkey
1976 Brunei
1977 Brazil
1978 United States of America
1979 Egypt
1980 Malaysia
1981 Japan
1982 Canada
1983 Sri Lanka
1984 Kenya
1985 Australia
1987 Soviet Union
1988 west coast of the USA
1989 Zimbabwe
1990 The Caribbean
1991 Japan
1992 Hungary and New Zealand
1993 Argentina
1994 New England, USA
1995 South Africa
1996 Hong Kong and China
1997 Canada
1998 Mexico

Above: When Valerie Singleton, John Noakes and Peter Purves were in Mexico, they went to see a Charreada. At the end of this thrilling horse show they were given huge sombrero hats and enormous horses and invited to show off their riding skills.

Tonga 1972

Above: In Tonga John Noakes, Peter Purves and Lesley Judd listened to local music while enjoying a mouth-watering spread of yams, pork, watermelon and sticky dumplings.
Below: Lesley Judd visited a dancing school in Bangkok, which has 1000 pupils aged ten and over. She found it incredibly difficult to follow the complicated steps of the intricate ritual of Thai dancing but had fun trying.

Thailand 1974

Brazil 1977

Left: *Blue Peter's first expedition to South America began in Rio de Janeiro. John Noakes climbed to the top of Corcovado mountain to see the statue of Christ the Redeemer and to enjoy the view.*

Egypt 1979

Below: *Simon Groom and Janet Ellis went on safari through Kenya's beautiful landscape. On the shores of Lake Baringo they met people of the Njemp tribe and Janet helped collect wood early in the morning.*

Kenya 1984

Above: *Christopher Wenner, Tina Heath and Simon Groom visited the biggest of the three pyramids at Giza and saw the mysterious Sphinx with a lion's body and man's face.*

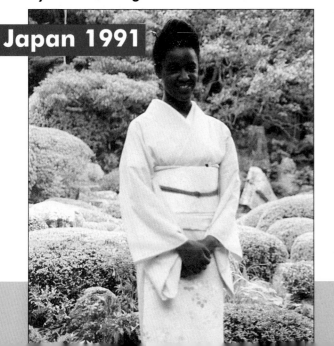

Below: *Diane-Louise Jordan dressed in a traditional Japanese kimono in one of Kyoto's famous gardens.*

Japan 1991

Soviet Union 1987

Above: *Yvette Fielding, Mark Curry and Caron Keating in Moscow's Red Square outside St Basil's Cathedral.*

Blue Peter *visits*

The Blue Peter team arrived in Canada on 1 July 1997 to begin a four-week marathon across the second largest country in the world. This was the thirty-second Summer Expedition and it would take Stuart, Katy, Romana and Richard on an unforgettable 5000-mile journey through mountains, deserts, past vast waterfalls, big cities and remote wildernesses, from Atlantic to Pacific – all part of a country that is big on dramatic contrasts.

The first day in July was a good day to arrive because not only was the nation celebrating Canada Day but it also saw the arrival of the ship "The Matthew" in St John's harbour, Newfoundland – the most easterly province of this vast country. "The Matthew" was a full-size replica of a ship of that name that had made an epic voyage from Britain across the Atlantic to Canada exactly 500 years before. John Cabot sailed from Bristol in 1497 and now that same journey had been retraced. Cabot's journey was important because it triggered the migration to Canada of European settlers, especially from Britain and France. It was especially exciting to watch the ship's arrival as Stuart had been in Bristol less than two months before to wave "The Matthew" off. In St John's harbour Richard was welcomed on board to celebrate the voyage and congratulate the crew.

The team's next port of call was Montreal, home to singer Celine Dion, in the French-speaking province of Quebec.

A quarter of Canadians have French ancestors, as for 200 years the British and French both had colonies in Canada. The British won the power battle against their French rivals but they have never won the language battle in Quebec – and the Quebecois are still very proud of their French traditions. Richard checked out Montreal's amazing underground city and got a taste for French Canadian life.

Katy and Richard then got the heebie-jeebies when they had a ride to the top of the world's tallest, free-standing structure in Toronto, Canada's largest city. The CN Tower is 555 metres tall and boasts a glass floor you can stand on – not for those without a head for heights. Meanwhile Romana took to the streets to check out Toronto's famous fashion scene and to visit a museum totally dedicated to shoes. She even donated a pair of her own – Romana's taste in footwear had now achieved international fame!

WE ARE HERE!

Right: *The team arrives in Toronto, Canada's largest city, and takes in the sights from the top of the CN Tower – a perfect way to get your bearings while enjoying a bite to eat in the revolving restaurant.*

CANADA

THE ROCKIES

CANADA

St John's

Québec

Calgary

Vancouver

Toronto   Montréal

USA

PACIFIC OCEAN

ATLANTIC OCEAN

Sport is huge in Canada and no one can leave Toronto without a visit to the world-famous Skydome to watch the even more famous Blue Jays baseball team. The Skydome, which has an amazing sliding roof, is also a hotel so Katy and Stuart were able to catch the game from the comfort of a hotel room.

Close to Toronto are the dramatic Niagara Falls. It poured with rain the day the team visited but it didn't really matter – the Falls soaked them anyway! Next they travelled on to the vast snow-capped Rocky Mountains in Calgary, home to the Calgary Stampede. The day Blue Peter arrived the city had

Top: *Katy, Stuart, Romana and Richard make a fashion statement Niagara-style during their visit to the spectacular Falls (centre).*
Bottom: *Western Canada is cowboy country so Katy and Richard try their hands at being ranch hands. "Yahoo!"*

Left: *Stuart, at the Banff National Park, about to go in search of Canada's famous wildlife.*

gone cowboy-crazy. Stuart and Katy donned their Stetsons, yelled "Yahoo" and learned what it takes to be a real cowboy.

Up in the stunning Rocky Mountains, Blue Peter went camping, but not with tents – oh no. The team got to grips with what the Canadians call an RV or Recreational Vehicle. It's basically a campervan the size of a coach containing every mod con, but driving it through the winding mountain roads was not for the fainthearted, as Katy discovered.

The Banff National Park is in the heart of the Rockies and contains some of the best wildlife in the world, including bears, wolves, eagles and moose. Stuart was lucky enough to take part in a scientific survey to radio-track wild animals from a helicopter. He actually got to see a grizzly bear mother with her two cubs close up. Awesome!

By the time they'd reached the beautiful city of Vancouver on the Pacific coast, the team had crossed the entire country. Canada's vast and beautiful landscapes, which are scarcely touched by mankind, had not disappointed.

Above: *It's tiring, this filming ... a long drive through the Rockies in a campervan.*

Right: *Vancouver – the final destination in the Blue Peter cross-Canada Summer Expedition.*

Chocolate treat!

Torrone Molle is sometimes called fridge cake and is simple to make although its ingredients aren't cheap. If you have a special occasion coming up and want to create something deliciously different to impress your friends and relatives try this Italian cake. Cut it into thin slices or small squares as it's rich and crunchy and a little goes a long, long way.

Here's how you make it

Prepare a cake or loaf tin for the Torrone Molle by lining it with cling film. This will make the cake easier to remove once it is finished.

Now to the cooking proper. Place the butter and cocoa powder in a clean mixing bowl and, using a large spoon, beat them together until they are well blended, smooth and creamy. Then mix in the ground almonds. In a saucepan, dissolve the sugar in a little water over a low heat and add to the mixture. Pour in the honey, stirring really well. Finally fold in the broken biscuits before putting the mixture into the prepared tin. Press the mixture firmly into the corners of the tin and level the top with a spatula. Cover with cling film and put in the fridge for at least four hours.

Take the Torrone Molle out of the fridge, just before you're ready to serve. For an extra special occasion, decorate it with whole almonds or crystallised violets.

Here's what you need
150g unsalted butter
150g cocoa powder
150g ground almonds
150g granulated sugar
water
1 tablespoon honey
150g Petit Beurre biscuits broken into small pieces

THIS CAKE CONTAIN NUTS SO MAKE SURE THAT IT IS NOT EATEN BY ANYONE WITH AN ALLERGY TO NUTS.

Diving belle

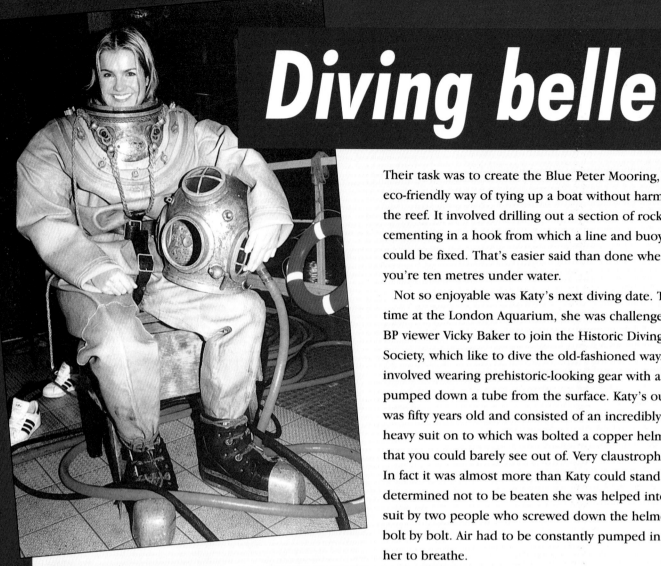

K aty has spent a busy year under water! Since getting her diving qualification, several Blue Peter challenges have involved getting wet …

Her first assignment was in 1997, which was the International Year of the Reef – a campaign to draw attention to the vulnerable undersea ecosystems. The living coral reefs that grow throughout the world's oceans are under attack from pollution, careless divers and boats dropping anchor and tearing at the coral.

Katy travelled to the Cayman Islands in the Caribbean Sea to find out more about the reef and what could be done to protect it. After taking a course in reef-friendly diving, she took part in a world-wide survey. Using a pen and waterproof paper, she monitored the spectacular variety of fish and plant life that live in and around the reef. "The most wonderful part for me was diving among rays that measured a metre across. As I knelt on the sea bed, they came over and played – it was superb," Katy marvelled.

The following day Katy and fellow diver Mike Grundy took the plunge, carrying drills and cement.

Their task was to create the Blue Peter Mooring, an eco-friendly way of tying up a boat without harming the reef. It involved drilling out a section of rock and cementing in a hook from which a line and buoy could be fixed. That's easier said than done when you're ten metres under water.

Not so enjoyable was Katy's next diving date. This time at the London Aquarium, she was challenged by BP viewer Vicky Baker to join the Historic Diving Society, which like to dive the old-fashioned way. This involved wearing prehistoric-looking gear with air pumped down a tube from the surface. Katy's outfit was fifty years old and consisted of an incredibly heavy suit on to which was bolted a copper helmet that you could barely see out of. Very claustrophobic! In fact it was almost more than Katy could stand, but determined not to be beaten she was helped into the suit by two people who screwed down the helmet bolt by bolt. Air had to be constantly pumped in for her to breathe.

Looking like a spaceman, the suit was unbearably heavy until she entered the water. Once underneath, it was really quite pleasant. She was able to speak because inside the helmet was a communication system wired to the surface. After fifteen minutes of walking about on the bottom checking out the fish, which included a close encounter with a conger eel, she resurfaced. "It's amazing to me that divers used to stay under water for up to ten hours in one of these," she said. Each to his or her own!

Katy goes under

Right: *Tim Vincent and Katy prepare for their first open-water dive before swimming with seals at the Farne Islands off the Northumberland coast.* **Opposite left:** *Katy dressed in a fifty-year-old Siebe Gorman Standard Dress before her dive at the London Aquarium.*

Opposite left: *Katy helps to build the environmentally-friendly Blue Peter Mooring in the Cayman Islands.*

Above left, centre and right: *Katy gets friendly with a fish at Sting Ray City in the Cayman Islands, where the rays like to come and play with the divers.*

STONE ME!

One of Stuart's more unusual assignments was to become a living statue. Here he describes the odd sensation of being turned into stone for the afternoon.

"I thought it was a wind-up when I heard I was going to be turned into a living statue live on air. But it was no joke! Apparently posh parties and celebrity events have been littered with live statues as the latest fashion 'must have'.

"I wanted to see photos and wasn't a bit surprised to find that all the live statues were a chip off Arnie Schwarzenegger's block.

"I gamely agreed to allow make-up artist Malin Coleman to cover my body with a white base coat. It was a water-based make-up and dried really quickly. Next she sponged and brushed the detail and shading on my torso – my pecs started to look quite respectable although I wasn't looking forward to my face and hair being turned into stone.

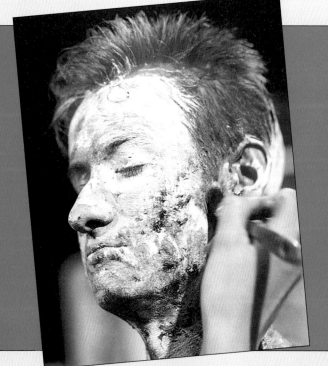

The make-up was cold and the brushes tickled my ears – I hardly dared breathe in case my face cracked. I imagine it's a bit like having a face pack: your facial muscles become frozen.

46

"While Malin added the finishing touches I asked the professionals about the perks of the job. Apparently many partygoers are completely fooled by the live statues and have been known to lean against them. Living statues also spend many an evening eavesdropping on juicy gossip. It seems like rather a good job but standing still with a straight face for up to an hour and a half? Believe me, it isn't easy – but a good idea for a fancy dress party!"

47

International

Space Station

Above: Computer graphic of what the International Space Station will look like in orbit.

Below: *To get a whole space station into orbit, you need something big, strong and reliable – the Space Shuttle. "It's impossible to imagine the noise and heat of blast-off," said Stuart, standing on the actual launch pad at the Kennedy Space Centre.*

Opposite top: *Node 1, a section of the International Space Station, being prepared for launch in a "clean room".*
Opposite centre: *An astronaut rehearses fitting together Space Station parts while weightless underwater.*
Opposite below: *The Neutral Buoyancy Lab pool is said to be the largest in the world.*
Opposite bottom: *Katy gets strapped in for her simulated journey into space.*

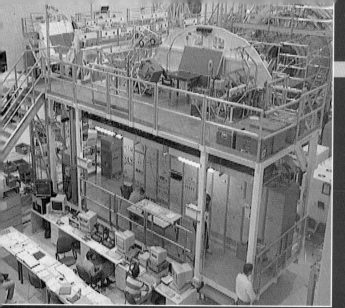

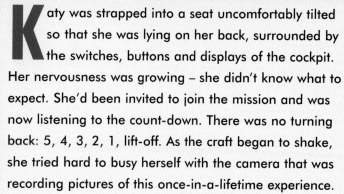

Katy was strapped into a seat uncomfortably tilted so that she was lying on her back, surrounded by the switches, buttons and displays of the cockpit. Her nervousness was growing – she didn't know what to expect. She'd been invited to join the mission and was now listening to the count-down. There was no turning back: 5, 4, 3, 2, 1, lift-off. As the craft began to shake, she tried hard to busy herself with the camera that was recording pictures of this once-in-a-lifetime experience.

Okay, so it wasn't a *real* lift-off but a simulated one of a Shuttle blasting off on a journey into space. Try convincing yourself that, however, when all your senses tell you it's the real thing. If you are an astronaut training for a Shuttle mission, such a simulated journey into space is a regular experience but it is unheard of if you're a television presenter. Forty-five minutes later, the crew conducted a textbook emergency landing and Katy emerged – shaken but not stirred – from the Shuttle simulator. She was greeted by four-times Shuttle astronaut and friend of Blue Peter, Marsha Ivins.

Katy, Stuart and Richard were in America to report on the most ambitious space programme undertaken since man landed on the Moon in July 1969. The International Space Station will be the largest structure ever to be sent into space. When completed, it will cover the size of two football pitches and will orbit at 17,500 m.p.h., some 248 nautical miles above Earth. At such a height, scientists in its six laboratories will be able to conduct experiments free from Earth's atmosphere. From their vantage point, they will be able to observe our planet and see amongst other things what condition it's in. The project is truly international with Europe, Russia, Japan, Canada and the USA all involved.

At NASA's Johnson Space Centre in Houston, Texas, Richard saw how astronauts are being specially trained to assemble the Space Station while in space. For this, the centrepiece is the Neutral Buoyancy Lab, a giant pool where underwater conditions are created to mimic the sensations of being in space.

Stuart got close up to some sections of the Space Station being readied for lift-off at the Kennedy Space Centre in Florida. "Standing on the actual launch pad where countless rockets have blasted into space is awesome," said Stuart. Some of the first sections of the Space Station are to be launched into space from that very spot from summer 1998, and the entire project is due for completion by 2002.

Pot it!

**Even if you haven't got
a garden or think you
haven't got green fingers,
you can still grow plants.**

The next time you're eating an
orange or squeezing a **lemon** or
lime, keep the pips. These seeds
may grow into plants. All you
need do is fill a small flowerpot
with potting compost, space out the
pips, cover with more compost, water
and leave on a sunny windowsill for
the tiny shoots to appear.

Peanuts, still in their shell (not roasted or salted), are also worth trying to grow. Simply crack one side of the peanut shell and pot in the same way as fruit pips. This time cover the pot with cling film, which helps keep in moisture and encourages growth. Once you see green shoots, remove the cling film. Leave the plant to grow in a warm sunny position in a humid atmosphere.

Pineapple tops, too, can grow into terrific-looking houseplants, so don't put them on the compost heap or in the bin. Mix equal quantities of sand and potting compost and fill a pot. Put the pineapple piece on top and cover the fleshy part with more potting compost. Water well, cover with a plastic bag and tie it at the top. After a week or two, the pineapple should sprout from the middle and you should then remove the plastic bag.

Sunflower seeds can be sown indoors or out in a sunny sheltered place in March or April. Once you've planted the seeds, water and protect them by covering the spot with the cut-off bottom half of a clear plastic drinks bottle. When the seedlings appear, pull out all but the strongest one, keeping it watered and supported with a bamboo cane as it grows taller. You could end up with a whopper in six months. Each year Blue Peter organises the tallest sunflower competition. Keep your tape measure handy as next year's winner could be green-fingered you!

5.54 metres tall!

Right: *The tallest sunflower, at 5.54 metres, ever recorded in our annual competition was grown in 1987 by Luke and Guy Mayhew against the back wall of their home in Kent.*

WEATHER PLANE

In December 1997, government leaders from all over the world gathered in Kyoto, Japan for a conference about climate change. They were trying to reach agreement on reducing the emission of "greenhouse" gases. Greenhouse gases are those that come from the burning of fossil fuels, such as car exhausts and power station emissions, as well as methane from farm animals, and chlorofluorocarbons (CFCs) used in refrigerators and aerosols. Together, these gases create the "greenhouse effect" and may be causing the climate to change.

Snoopy flies at heights of 7000 to 10,000 metres and flights can last anything from three to twelve hours.

Some scientists believe that climate change is possibly the greatest threat facing life on Earth. Climate change can mean the warming of the planet (often called "global warming") or the cooling of the climate. Either way, this may have huge effects on the planet and its species.

Stuart went to visit some of the people who think they know what may really be happening to our climate, because they measure the greenhouse effect with a special aeroplane called Snoopy. The Meteorological Research Flight use this converted Hercules as a flying laboratory. "I've never seen a plane with so many things sticking out of it," said Stuart looking at Snoopy's probes, including the long nose at the front, which keeps some instruments away from aircraft turbulence. The various instruments absorb samples of air, which they measure for gases such as ozone, CFCs and carbon dioxide, while lasers monitor cloud droplets and the pollution within them.

Top: *On some days the surrounding pollution becomes visible in the atmosphere, creating an unhealthy haze of smog.*
Above: *Cloud formations are very complicated because no two clouds are identical.*

climate and the world's weather systems is far from clear. More pollution may mean the atmosphere is getting warmer but with more clouds it could mean that more of the sun's rays will be reflected back into the upper atmosphere with the result that the climate may cool.

Meanwhile it's important for us to reduce pollution from factory chimneys and to develop alternatives to the petrol engine in order to keep global warming under control. Snoopy will continue to help scientists measure whether we're being successful or not.

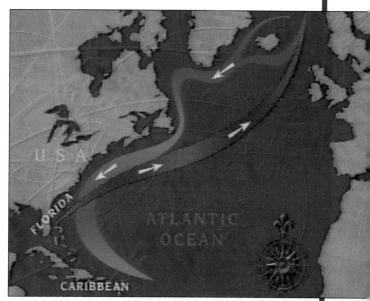

Snoopy's advantage is its size, allowing a team of scientists to do several different experiments on each flight and to change their research as the weather varies. When in flight, the scientists ask the pilot to go wherever the clouds look interesting.

Clouds develop when water droplets form around tiny particles of dust or dirt in the atmosphere. Some dust – like that from volcanic eruptions – is natural but some is due to pollution. Snoopy analyses clouds and the air surrounding them.

The results are sent to the Meteorological Office in Bracknell, Berkshire for detailed analysis. There, at the Centre for Climate Prediction, huge computers find out if the world's climate really is changing and predict the effects of global warming. The scientists look at how clouds and the movement and temperature of ocean currents, such as El Niño in the Pacific and the Gulf Stream in the Atlantic, might affect the climate.

Some scientists think that they have enough information to prove that global warming is a reality, but, even if this were true, the effect on

Top: *Shifts in the direction of ocean currents like the Gulf Stream may make Britain, for example, cooler than it is now.*
Above: *Snoopy is jammed full of scientific instruments that analyse and observe the content and behaviour of the atmosphere. Thousands of recordings are made during each flight.*

CIRQUE DU SOLEIL

World-famous Cirque du Soleil were in the middle of a European tour when Richard and Katy caught up with them in Dusseldorf, Germany. They were invited to join the troupe on an amazing behind-the-scenes experience, where they met the stars, learned all about circus life and had a bit of a go, too … it's harder than it looks!

Cirque du Soleil is no ordinary circus. It has performed in more than 118 cities around the world and entertained more than ten million spectators since it was founded in Quebec (Canada) in 1984.

Travelling with a truly international cast and crew from twenty-one different countries, Cirque du Soleil's latest show Alegria was touring twelve cities in seven countries when Katy and Richard joined them. They were about to pack up 800 tons of equipment in their forty-two trailers and head from Dusseldorf to London for a month performing at the Royal Albert Hall.

Alegria is a Spanish word expressing elation, joy and jubilation, and the show conjures up the atmosphere of the days when family circuses travelled across Europe. Characters in costume and make-up resembling court jesters mingle on stage and in the audience to "introduce" a magical performance by acrobats, aerial artists, clowns, contortionists and fire dancers. For Alegria alone, ninety costumes had to be created (that's a lot of ironing as Katy found …) in addition to numerous headpieces, masks and 400 pairs of shoes.

The cast of fifty-four range in age from five to

Left: *The show is a stunning mix of drama, dance, theatre, mime, music and circus skills.*
Right: *During two months of training in Las Vegas, Paul Bowler learned the "cube" act from the only other person in the world who does it. It's a truly strenuous act, which he performs at ten metres above the ground. Paul gave Katy a few tips in mid-air on how to stop the cube from dropping.*

fifty-five. The only Brit in the show is twenty-nine-year-old, ex-Olympic gymnast Paul Bowler, from Manchester. After competing in the Barcelona Olympics, but failing to qualify for Atlanta, he joined Cirque du Soleil. Paul's speciality is the "cube" act, which is really amazing to watch.

Another spectacular act is the Russian bars. Two people hold the bar while a gymnast on the bar is flung several metres into the air before landing back on the bar. A truly magical moment is when one of the circus children climbs into the arms of an adult on the bar, who then performs a somersault – definitely not something to try at home!

Among the children in the show are two thirteen-year-olds, Nomean and Otchki from Mongolia, who perform an extraordinary contortion duet bending their bodies into shapes that are almost unbelievable. It's as though their bones are made of rubber.

Richard later met up with the girls in the Cirque school, which they attend every day along with the other children from the circus. The school follows the French Canadian system of education so all the lessons are in French. Most of the children speak three languages – French, English and their own mother tongue – so they're top-class academics as well as acrobats!

Blooming gorgeous gifts

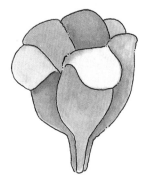

You will need

Card, 7 x 11cm, for petal pattern
Coloured tissue paper (such as
paper table napkins, gift-wrap tissue
or handkerchief tissues) for the petals
Contrasting coloured thin paper
for the petal centres
Sticky tape
Drinking straw (preferably bendy) for stem
Green crepe paper or any thin paper
coloured green
Paper glue
Paper or plastic cup, plastic flower pot,
tiny milk portion or yoghurt tub
Paint for pot (white emulsion paint
and coloured paints)
Newspaper to fill pot
Green paper or pot scourer to
cover newspaper

The flower petals

1 To make a pattern for the petals, fold the card in half lengthways and draw a curved line across the bottom open corner.

2 Cut away the card outside the drawn line.

3 Open out the card and you should have a filled-in U-shape for each petal.

4 Fold the coloured tissue paper so that you can cut out several petals at once.

5 Lay your pattern on it and draw around the pattern with a pencil. Cut out the petals.

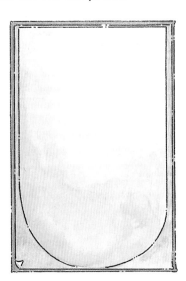

6 Bunch the straight ends of the petals together – six to eight petals should be enough to make a flower. Squeeze the bunched ends together tightly and wind a piece of sticky tape around them. You can then spread out the petals so that the flower is a good shape.

The flower stem

1 Attach the bendy end of the straw to the bunched ends of the flower with some sticky tape.

2 Cover the straw with a strip of green paper, securing the end of the green paper strip with a little glue over the bunched end of the flower.

3 Then wind the strip all down the length of the straw, cut off any spare paper and glue the very end to stop it unwinding again.

The leaves

1 Cut out two or three leaf shapes from green paper.

2 Glue one end of each leaf around the stem about a third of the way up from the end of the straw.

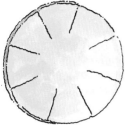 

The flower centre

1 Cut out each flower centre from two circles of thin paper in a contrasting colour to the petals.
2 Keeping the layers together, make short cuts into the circles all around.
3 Pinch in the middle and give a little twist and then glue the twisted bit into the middle of your flower.

The flower pot

1 Give the pot a coat of white emulsion, remembering to paint a little way down inside the pot as that will still show when the flower is in place.
2 Then paint the pot with a different colour.
3 When the coloured paint is dry, paint on a pattern, matching it to one of the flower colours.
4 Stuff some crumpled newspaper into the pot, leaving some space at the top.

5 Push a pencil down through the centre of the newspaper to make a hole for the flower stem.
6 Insert the flower stem into the hole and cover the newspaper with strands of cut-up paper. Alternatively, cut out a circle of green pot scourer to fit the pot, cut a hole in the centre for the flower stem and place the scourer on the newspaper. Push the flower stem through the scourer hole and into the newspaper.

PARACHUTE RECORD BREAKERS

"They've given me the greatest experience of my life, and I'll never stop being grateful." That's how John Noakes described his record-breaking jump in May 1973, when he became the first civilian in Britain to make a 5 mile high, free-fall parachute jump as well as the first "outsider" to join the RAF Flying Falcons. At 5 miles (8000 metres) above the earth, there is very little oxygen so John had to learn how to use breathing apparatus as well as how to train for the big jump itself.

On the big day, the team took off from RAF Abingdon to the dropping zone over Salisbury Plain in Wiltshire. There were eleven Falcons plus John, who was No. 1, the first out of the plane. Once out, John linked up for the free fall with three other team members, one of whom was wearing a helmet camera. That was another first: John Noakes was the first television presenter in Britain to talk to a camera while falling through space. The free fall lasted about 7000 metres – the parachute opening at 1000 metres. His achievement won a place in *The Guinness Book of Records*.

Janet Ellis's big day came in October 1986, when a jump from 6100 metres created a European-record, free-fall jump for a civilian woman. A year before, Janet had broken her pelvis in training from a static-line jump but, with huge determination, was back training with the Falcons six months later. Now on this her final jump, Janet was to do 1½ minutes in free fall before pulling the ripcord at 1200 metres to release the parachute. Steering her canopy towards the dropping-zone target, Janet achieved one of her best landings, hitting the ground only a couple of metres from the target. Janet held the record for six months until it was broken by Valerie Slattery and Francesca Gannon jumping from 7600 metres, in March 1987. "I wouldn't have missed it for the world," said Janet, even though it had taken 3½ years of training, thirty-three jumps and a broken pelvis!

In 1994, Stuart took up the Blue Peter free-falling tradition by teaming up once again with the Falcons so that he could take part in a Falcons' Display. As well as training in Britain, Stuart also went with the team to the USA for some spectacular jumping over the California Desert in 1996. In a practice display, he jumped out of a Hercules with the Falcons to create a ten-man stack.

To celebrate the 3000th edition of Blue Peter, in May 1997, Stuart and Katy did a simultaneous, tandem, parachute drop on to a special BP 3000 target. As a safety precaution, they couldn't actually jump together – the BP team considering them much too valuable!

Finally Stuart achieved his full ambition and in doing so went into the history books as the first civilian to take part in a full public display with the Falcons at the Biggin Hill Air Show, in June 1997. "As I stood at the back of the plane waiting for the green light I had big butterflies in my stomach because I didn't want anything to go wrong for me or the team." Fortunately, the free fall and linking up with members of the Falcons in the stack all went well. Flying the Blue Peter flag as he landed, Stuart was almost spot on the target.

Opposite top left: *John Noakes in mid free fall.*
Opposite top right: *Janet Ellis suspended by a harness, learning the free-fall position.*
Top left: *Stuart joining up in mid-air with members of RAF Flying Falcons.*
Above: *In the bay of a Hercules plane, Stuart with the entire Falcons team.*

Above: *A last-minute briefing – no turning back now for Stuart.*
Left: *Stuart during his historic display at Biggin Hill in 1997.*

Opposite centre: *Stuart and Katy after a safe landing, following their tandem jump to mark the 3000th edition of Blue Peter in May 1997.*

A RIDE TO REMEMBER

"Wild horses wouldn't keep me away," exclaimed Katy when told about her next filming assignment. However as she approached the New Forest she wondered if she had bitten off more than she could chew …

Katy was due to take part in an event that was guaranteed to test her courage and strength to its limits. The New Forest Pony Drift is an annual spectacle that's as old as the Forest itself. Every autumn the ponies that live wild in the New Forest are rounded up for a health check, and the Drift involves tearing over miles of countryside chasing these ponies into a corral, where they are wormed, branded and examined. But rounding up animals scattered throughout the forest is no mean feat. The only way to do the job is on horseback and, as Katy was to find out, it was going to be a ride to remember.

As she mounted her horse she knew that she had to trust him completely – he knew the land amazingly well and she wasn't familiar with it at all. From the very start it was a fast and furious ride. "I'm holding on for dear life … My horse has the cheeky habit of jumping gorse bushes without any warning," screamed Katy as she galloped past – but she was at least managing to stay in the saddle.

Three hours later the ponies had been successfully rounded up and the horses that had chased them were sweating and tired out. Katy, too, was exhausted and her hands were raw and blistered from the effort of holding on to the reins. "It was absolutely amazing, the best! Just my kind of riding – galloping for miles and miles in beautiful countryside. It was completely exhilarating. I've discovered muscles I didn't know I had – and I need a good hot bath!"

Top left: *Katy getting to know her horse Bruno.*
Above centre: *Tearing over the open countryside of the New Forest was exciting but required all the concentration Katy could muster.*
Above: *Three of the New Forest ponies being successfully rounded up.*

How to win your
Blue Peter
BADGE

There are five types of badges – Blue, Silver, Green, Competition and Gold – so why *not* try your hand at winning at least one of them.

Blue badges are the ones the presenters usually wear. You could win one for sending us an idea for the programme, an interesting letter, recipe, picture, poem or story. If you ever take part in the programme, this is the badge you'll be awarded. Like all our badges, it entitles you to free entry to nearly 200 attractions all over Britain. When you win your Blue Peter badge, we'll send you a list of all these places. You must wear your badge when you visit one, though.

Silver badges are awarded to people who have already won a Blue badge. You have to do something different to win it, so if you won your Blue badge for sending a good idea for the programme, you could draw a picture or make up a recipe to win a Silver.

Green badges are our environmental awards. If you tell us about an environmental project, write a poem, a song or give us your views about any "green" subject, you could win a Green badge. Let us know what you have been doing to help the world around you.

Gold badges are our highest award. They are rare and only awarded to people for outstanding bravery and courage or for representing your country in an international event. You can't "earn" a gold badge by winning all our others.

Competition badges are awarded to winners and runners-up. You have more chance than you might think of winning one of these so keep those entries coming in!

Answers to the Blue Peter 40th birthday challenge

1 Canada

2 The Marathon

3 Barnacle Bill

4 John Leslie, Romana D'Annunzio

5 Goldie

6 Biddy Baxter

7 John Noakes

8 Silver birch

9 John Noakes

10 Tortoise

11 Jason

12 Peter Purves

13 Lulu

14 A flag

15 Concorde

16 Konnie Huq

17 3000th edition

18 Argentina

19 Sarah Greene

20 Richard Bacon

Published in Great Britain in 1998 by World International Ltd, Deanway Technology Centre, Wilmslow Road, Handforth, Cheshire SK9 3FB.
Printed in Italy ISBN 0 7498 3761 6

Our address is: Blue Peter, BBC TV Centre, London W12 7RJ

Our home page is: http://www.bbc.uk/bluepeter
e-mail: bluepeter@bbc.co.uk